Missing You

By E.B. Allen

Dedication

For all the people I loved and lost in this life... a part of me will always miss you.

CONTENTS

I could write a thousand beautiful words about you, but it will never change the darkness you carry in your heart. I could love you for a million heartbeats, but you will never love me back. I could tear my world apart from pain, but it will never bring you back.

ACKNOWLEDGMENTS

A special thank you to every person who believed in me…
loved me… let me be welcomed into their world. Even if
for just a brief moment in time. I thank you all.

A fragile moment of pain and silence
I reach for the dream of you
Still lingering in my mind
I feel sorrow and darkness
Sinking deep inside my soul
Realizing you are gone
From the depths of my world
No longer fulfilling my desires
My bed feels haunted and empty

You were a bandit
And I was just another train
Passing by
That you needed to pillage

The sky was an empty space in the night. A scribe wrote poetry and beauty with each star created above. Humanity soon forgets about the darkness and sees only light as each star tells a story of love and loss.

Wither away with me as we turn to dust and allow flowers to grow from our bones.

Let's be fragile together
In the wounds of our broken souls
We can find a hiding place to run to
A place just for us
We can feel safe from the harshness
Of the cold world that hurt us
Maybe we can even find each other
In the vast darkness of our minds

I will leave the light on in this darkness for you to maybe find your way back to me someday.

Some people pass through your life causing a small ripple while others create a tsunami inside your soul. You have to decide if it will destroy you or if you will let it just return to being part of the beautiful ocean within you.

Someday someone will understand me, and I won't need to hide my demons.

As long as I am breathing, I will remember your sweet kisses. I will always want your tongue and mine to find each other in the dark.

You are lovely, and I want to keep you close
to me.

Every time you leave, I feel like pulling you back into bed with me and never letting you go. I want you to stay forever but I know you have to leave.

I will want to be with you for a thousand days and then I will want you to be forever after that. I'm not sure you can handle the forever...

I feel like it is safer to just run away because I am wanting way more than you and that is never a good feeling.

Everything feels better when I am in your arms. I miss you way more than I should when you are gone.

The heart breaks for the wrong ones just as
it does for the right ones. Letting go of
someone you let inside your world is never
easy.

A piece of me died that day. I cannot ever awaken it again. I have tried to breathe life back into it, but it is gone. I will never be the same.

You stained my blood with your touch. I will forever bleed you out as poems to try and heal my broken soul.

It is a sweet pain that rips my heart open
whenever I think about you.

Peoples paths cross for a reason. Ours did too. Maybe they will cross again someday, but even if they don't... you were my favorite distraction from my chaotic life.

So many people claim to be able to handle the darkness, but they always run away in the end.

You will never be seen as a waste of my time. My soul is very powerful and a very loving force... you took a part of me with you. For that reason alone, I am happy to have known you.

Maybe you will find me in the darkness still waiting.

I dreamt you kissed me once again. I woke up to an echo of pain inside my heart. Screaming out for silence to take away this darkness pulling me into pieces.

Silence only proves what we already know
but we keep hoping that it doesn't.

Her mind comes to terms with a broken
heart while her soul begs the universe to go
back in time for another chance with him.

I never expected you to love me. But I also never expected you to leave me so quickly.

I picture you so clearly in my mind, but you
are gone when I open my eyes.

Hide all of the darkness inside of me so the pain of his absence will fade away into the shadows.

His heart didn't break nearly as much as hers did. For she was easily replaced by him... but his void inside of her would never be filled in the same way.

It can be scary to think about losing you
But you are not really mine
No one belongs to anyone in this life
Yet I still want to keep you
All to myself as long as I can

I do not always wake up missing you. But it slowly crawls under my skin sinking into my veins... like a drug I want you so badly I would do anything for just a taste. You are my drug and I am a recovering addict.

I shall never stumble over the words you
spill out so sweetly. For you said goodbye
and I have regained my balance.

I danced with your ghost as we said
goodbye. It was the only part of you that
didn't want to see me go.

I had all but forgotten about you. Then she comes around to remind me. Who would have thought your ghosts would haunt me too.

In the distance, I found myself wanting everything that you were not. Goodbye was a chance to see you as you really were and not for who I wanted you to be.

It was as if a storm came through my soul and blew away all the parts of you that I loved... because I woke up one morning not missing you anymore. And on that day... my life began again with a fresh start at finding happiness.

Your love vanished into the ether before I even had a chance to kiss you goodbye.

Maybe it's not normal
This feeling of missing him
It burrows its poison
Into my dark veins
It taints my blood
And makes me question
My every thought
The beating of my heart
Carries him deeper inside
My pulse quickens
I scream out
In pleasure
And in agony
From this memory of him

I could write a thousand beautiful words about you, but it will never change the darkness you carry in your heart. I could love you for a million heartbeats, but you will never love me back. I could tear my world apart from pain, but it will never bring you back.

All my friends are ghosts
From pasts
Forgotten
But missed
Deeply
My soul aches
Thinking
Of each
And every
Fucking one
Of them

I would have sinned with you. Every day and every night. Until our bodies were merely bones. Won't you come back so I can show you how to do it right.

I called myself your friend
While you wanted to make me
A stranger

* when love ends

If I am so easily forgotten
Then I will slip away
From your memories
Until we become strangers
Yet again
In a sea of humanity
Where my face blurs
Among the chaos
And the ruins
Of your twisted mind
I seek nothing more from you now
Than to be forgotten
By you
Forever

I left you in the darkness
And the bitter cold of winter
A haunting feeling sits
Deep inside my chest
Where your head once slept
And my heart once beat faster
As if you were the one

I can feel myself growing colder
Two strangers turning stranger
Passing by time eternal
Whispering madness into existence
Like we have any power
Over this thing we call love
My veins screamed out for you
But you remain stranger still
And will forever more my love

If I could unwrite myself from your memory
and introduce myself as new... I would do
just that. Because I am not the same me
and you are not the same you. Maybe then
we would get it right.

Yesterday feels like a year and last year was another lifetime ago. My childhood feels like someone else's dream or even a nightmare at times. This life has been everlasting, yet I know one day it will end and my one regret will be never loving you.

Time should make things easier
But it's the song on the radio
The look on his face
As I pass him on the street
I'm not noticed in the slightest
So, my heart skips a beat
Then my mind goes dark
And he is gone
Just like before

I'm going to lose you
Again
As you slip through
My life
All of my favorite lies
The ones you told me
Time and time again
The ones my mind felt
But my heart felt more
Words like love and babe
Slips of the tongue
Resting carefully in my ear
As you speak and I fall
Deeper into losing you
Once again

My emotions have an echo
A return to time and space
Even my veins vibrate
In a world trying to remember
How you felt beside me

I have decided to leave my memories of you behind in a casket of velvet buried under a lilac tree deep in the dark forest of forgotten dreams. You were after all nothing but a dream.

Your soul flooded my world. I was drowning the moment we met. Always gasping for air as my lungs filled with your wants and desires. I tried to survive in your world, but I was not able to breathe. You would have killed me had I let you stay.

If I write about you enough... maybe my
mind will forget you exist.

I have not found a way to be here without you so I'm just going to let the days take me until there are no more.

It still amazes me that I was ever close enough to touch your heart. Even if it was only for a short time.

I let myself forget about you
For little moments in time
You are not here
Then something happens
A rush of you comes over me
Then I remember everything
Your smile
Your touch
Your silly hats
It was a brief affair
But the memories are so sweet

I tried to fill the void with you
I created a version of myself
Worthy of being loved by you
I miss that version of myself
The way I felt with you
Will never be replaced

It was a mistake to think
I could hold someone like you
Forever in my arms
To believe in a love everlasting
I wanted to hold you
But you only wanted to leave

I am not smooth
Nor easy to handle
You gave me peace
Then you gave me silence
Now you are gone

Gently resting in a place beneath my ribs is a heart that once beat for you. It carried a love deeper than the breaths my soul could take. And in that love affair my bones fell apart until the day you walked away. I finally understand how to breathe on my own so my bones can finally rest.

Deprived of loving you
My heart is lost
Where once I felt the ocean
I now feel the void

Choose yourself and feel how the loss of love helps you grow into the person you were meant to become.

I lost the battle to keep you
But I won the war to keep myself
Maybe the war of love keeps us alive
One day the battlefield will be filled
With daisies instead of bullets
And my heart will be filled with love
Instead of instead of loss

All of the days are numbered
I cannot recall them
But I know they are there
Taunting me with their existence
Knowing how long you have been gone
Feeling the weight of the sun
Rising each day
I settle with my thoughts
Of living life without you
For the rest of my days

You were different
Because I was different
I wanted to be loved
In all the ways I had not been before
I wanted something better
I am still waiting
On something better

I feel your breath resting on my skin
Each night while I sleep
And dream of you
Each night feels brand new
But morning feels the same
I miss the way you woke me
Gentle kisses
And a beautiful face

There was this broken promise
Played out by you
And then another
Then another
Each story the same
Love breaking
An already wounded heart

If your ache reaches out for me
I will embrace it
I will love it
I will surrender
And become one
With your pain

Such luscious bones
To be torn apart
By a villain like you
Beware the destroyer
Of souls and hearts
He is not a man
Nor lover
To anyone
But himself

I have fallen for lies
That turn into love
I have shed tears
That turn into love
I have found love
Places one should not
Seek out love at all

I waited to be seen by you
As an equal to be loved

You left me sinking
In the depth of your kisses
Every time you said goodbye
My lips pulsating
And desiring your touch
Once again to return to me

Sacrifice your hands
Give them over to my flesh
Leave me wanting
Waiting
For your sweet taste
Upon my lips

In my heart
You beat
In my body
You pulsate
In my mind
You radiate

I will keep blending my edges
As you fade deeper
Inside of me
Fingers glide down my spine
Moans linger in the darkness
Your luscious tip
Gently slides across my lips
Wet with the desire
Of feeling every inch
Sliding in and out
I gasp and scream
And awake from the dream

The end of everything... there is only silence.

ABOUT THE AUTHOR

EB Allen is a photographer and poet from the Midwest. They can most often be found behind either a camera lens or a computer screen. Visions of a better tomorrow are all that they wish for in this life. Thank you for reading and following along with the thoughts and ideas of EB Allen.